GOLDEN STATE
WARRIORS

**Sam Moussavi
and
Samantha Nugent**

AV² provides enriched content that supplements and complements this book. Weigl's AV² books strive to create inspired learning and engage young minds in a total learning experience.

Your AV² Media Enhanced books come alive with...

Audio
Listen to sections of the book read aloud.

Key Words
Study vocabulary, and complete a matching word activity.

Video
Watch informative video clips.

Quizzes
Test your knowledge.

Embedded Weblinks
Gain additional information for research.

Slide Show
View images and captions, and prepare a presentation.

Try This!
Complete activities and hands-on experiments.

... and much, much more!

Go to **www.av2books.com**, and enter this book's unique code.

BOOK CODE

N952232

AV² **by Weigl** brings you media enhanced books that support active learning.

Published by AV² by Weigl
350 5th Avenue, 59th Floor
New York, NY 10118
Website: www.av2books.com

Library of Congress Control Number: 2016935100

ISBN 978-1-4896-4689-7 (Hardcover)
ISBN 978-1-4896-4690-3 (Multi-user eBook)

Printed in the United States of America, in Brainerd, Minnesota
1 2 3 4 5 6 7 8 9 0 20 19 18 17 16

082016
200516

Project Coordinator Heather Kissock
Art Director Terry Paulhus

Photo Credits
Every reasonable effort has been made to trace ownership and to obtain permission to reprint copyright material. The publishers would be pleased to have any errors or omissions brought to their attention so that they may be corrected in subsequent printings.

Weigl acknowledges Newscom, Getty Images, and Alamy as its primary image suppliers for this title.

GOLDEN STATE WARRIORS

CONTENTS

Introduction

The Golden State Warriors play an exciting and hard-working style of basketball. On offense, players are free to move and shoot from anywhere on the floor. On defense, players help each other out and are aggressive for **rebounds**. However, it took a long time for the team to become successful.

The young, exciting players that make up the team are an important part of what is making the Golden State Warriors great. Point guard Stephen Curry is a perfect example of this. His outside shooting abilities are inspiring. Shooting guard Klay Thompson and power forward Draymond Green are also important players that are keeping the game in the Bay Area thrilling.

Shooting guard Klay Thompson was drafted in 2011 by the Golden State Warriors. In 2015, he was named an NBA All-Star.

The arrival of head coach Steve Kerr before the 2014–15 season marked a turning point for the team. What is most clear about today's Golden State Warriors is they play as a team and have fun doing it. The Warriors do not look to be slowing down either, as they aim to bring home yet another NBA Championship.

Point guard and shooting guard Shawn Livingston was drafted after graduating from high school in 2004. In 2014, he signed with the Golden State Warriors.

GOLDEN STATE WARRIORS

Arena Oracle Arena

Division Pacific Division (Western **Conference**)

Head Coach Steve Kerr

Location Oakland, California

NBA Championships 4 (1947, 1956, 1975, & 2015)

Nickname(s) "Dubs," GSW

6 Retired Numbers

70 Seasons

4 Division Titles

8 Conference Titles

32 Playoff Appearances

History

The Warriors franchise has had **25** head coaches in the team's history.

Andre Iguodala was instrumental to the Warriors' 2015 Finals title. He was named the NBA Finals MVP for his efforts.

The **franchise** was founded in 1946 as the Philadelphia Warriors. They played their first three seasons in the Basketball Association of America (BAA). The Warriors won the 1947 BAA Championship before joining the National Basketball Association (NBA) in the 1949 BAA-NBA Merger. The team stayed in Philadelphia for a total of 16 seasons and won the 1956 NBA Championship, the franchise's second title.

In 1962, the team moved to California and changed its name to the San Francisco Warriors. The Warriors made the **playoffs** five times in their nine seasons in San Francisco, including two NBA Finals appearances. Before the 1971–72 season, the franchise moved across San Francisco Bay to Oakland, California. Behind head Coach Al Attles and star Rick Barry, the Golden State Warriors won the 1975 NBA Championship.

For the next 30 seasons, the Warriors struggled to be successful. Led by Coach Don Nelson and point guard Baron Davis, the Warriors made a surprising run in the 2007 Playoffs. The team then rebuilt its roster by drafting young talent and by 2014, made the playoffs for two straight seasons. What followed was a historic 2014–15 season, capped by the franchise's fourth NBA Championship.

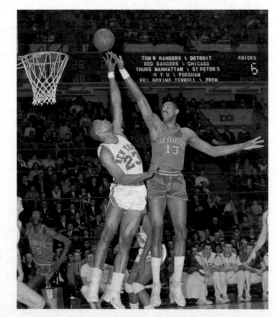

Basketball legend Wilt Chamberlain made his NBA debut with the Warriors. In his first game, the rookie Chamberlain put up 43 points against the New York Knicks.

The Arena

In 2008, 20,737 Warriors fans set a California record. They became the largest crowd to fill an arena to watch a basketball game in California history.

With a capacity of

19,596

fans, Oracle Arena is the largest NBA Arena in California.

The Philadelphia Warriors played at Philadelphia Arena from 1946 to 1962. From 1952 to 1962, the Warriors split their home games between the Philadelphia Convention Hall and the Philadelphia Arena. When the team moved west in 1962, it played at Cow Palace in Daly City, California, just south of San Francisco.

The Warriors played at Cow Palace until 1964. From 1964 to 1966, the team played at two different arenas in San Francisco. The first was Civic Auditorium in downtown San Francisco. The second was War Memorial Gymnasium on the University of San Francisco campus.

The team played at Cow Palace again from 1966 to 1971. Before the 1971–72 season, the Golden State Warriors moved into Coliseum Arena in Oakland and stayed there until 1996. While the Coliseum Arena was being renovated, the Warriors played one season at the San Jose Arena in San Jose, California. In 1997, the team moved back into Coliseum Arena and still plays its home games there. Today, Coliseum Arena is called Oracle Arena. Oracle is nicknamed "Roaracle" because of how loudly Warriors fan cheer at home games.

The Oracle's renovations between 1996 and 1997 cost $121 million.

Where They Play

Arena
Oracle Arena

Location
7000 Coliseum Way
Oakland, California 94621

Broke Ground
April 15, 1964

Completed
November 9, 1966

Features
• Seats 19,596
• Oldest NBA arena
• Eight theater boxes

LEGEND
☆ Oracle Arena
■ Western Conference
■ Eastern Conference

Newfoundland
Quebec
Prince Edward Island
New Brunswick
New Hampshire
Vermont
Maine
Nova Scotia
Massachusetts
Rhode Island
Connecticut
New York
New Jersey
Pennsylvania
Delaware
Maryland
District of Columbia
Michigan
Ohio
Indiana
West Virginia
Virginia
Kentucky
North Carolina
Tennessee
South Carolina
Alabama
Georgia
Florida
Atlantic Ocean
CANADA

N W E S

SOUTHEAST DIVISION
16. Atlanta Hawks
17. Charlotte Hornets
18. Miami Heat
19. Orlando Magic
20. Washington Wizards

CENTRAL DIVISION
21. Chicago Bulls
22. Cleveland Cavaliers
23. Detroit Pistons
24. Indiana Pacers
25. Milwaukee Bucks

ATLANTIC DIVISION
26. Boston Celtics
27. Brooklyn Nets
28. New York Knicks
29. Philadelphia 76ers
30. Toronto Raptors

The Uniforms

3 The Warriors played three games in their **"Chinese New Year"** uniforms during the 2015–16 season.

The Warriors' colors of gold, blue, and white are also California's state colors. Schools and universities, such as the University of California, Berkley, also widely use the colors.

From 1946 to 1962, the Philadelphia Warriors used blue, red, and gold as their colors. Both the white and blue uniforms read "Phila." When the team moved to California in 1962, the uniforms remained the same except for replacing "Phila" with "San Francisco" across the chest.

In 1964, the franchise adopted blue and gold as its colors. Until 1966, both the gold home and blue away uniforms read "Warriors." The team then used variations of "The City" design from 1966 to 1989. The most popular design of this era had "The City" above a **logo** of the Oakland Bay Bridge on both the home and away uniforms. The Warriors used navy blue, gold, and orange as its colors starting in 1997. That design existed until 2010, when the team returned to the Bay Bridge design of the late 1960s. The Warriors currently use this design.

HOME

AWAY

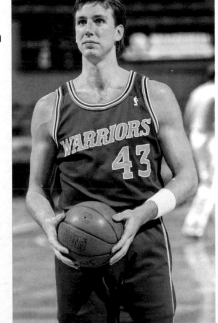

During the 1990s, the Warriors opted for a more conventional NBA uniform design, with the team name written across the chest.

The Coaches

The Warriors won **73** games during the 2015–16 season, under the direction of Steve Kerr.

Before coaching, Steve Kerr played in the NBA. He won three championships with Michael Jordan and the Chicago Bulls, along with two more championships with the San Antonio Spurs.

O f the Golden State Warriors 25 head coaches, 12 have led the franchise to the NBA Playoffs. Coaches Edward Gottlieb, George Senesky, Al Attles, and Steve Kerr have won NBA Championships. Former NBA players, such as Mark Jackson, Bill Sharman, Don Nelson, and George Senesky, have also served as Warriors coaches.

AL ATTLES Before coaching, Al Attles played in the NBA for 11 seasons. He became head coach of the San Francisco Warriors during the 1969–70 season. Attles coached the Warriors until 1983. He is the franchise leader in coaching wins, with 557. Attles also added 31 playoff wins to his record. He led the Warriors to the 1975 NBA title, the franchise's third.

DON NELSON Don Nelson coached the Warriors on two separate occasions. Once was from 1988 to 1995 and the second time was from 2006 to 2010. Nelson is second on the coaching wins list, with 442. He led the franchise to the NBA playoffs in 5 of his 11 seasons with Golden State. Nelson also served as head coach to the Milwaukee Bucks, New York Knicks, and Dallas Mavericks.

STEVE KERR Steve Kerr became the Warriors' head coach before the 2014–15 season. In his first season, he led the team to the 2015 NBA Title. Making this even more impressive is the fact that Kerr had no head coaching experience before taking over in Golden State.

The Mascot

Thunder's costume design was based off of the Warriors' redesigned logo. The team used the blue warrior with a lightning bolt on his head between 1997 and 2010.

The Golden State Warriors do not currently have a mascot. The last time the Warriors had a mascot was during the 2007–08 season. That mascot's name was Thunder, a superhero dressed in navy blue, wearing a Warriors jersey. Thunder was removed as the team's mascot before the 2008–09 season because Oklahoma City's basketball team was already named "Thunder."

After being removed as the team's official mascot, Thunder disappeared from the Bay Area. While the Warriors were in China for a series of preseason games in 2013, Thunder appeared at one of the exhibition games. It was the first time anyone had seen Thunder since he left the team in 2008.

fun facts

#1 The Golden States Warriors are currently one of the five teams in the NBA that do not have a mascot.

#2 Thunder was one of the few mascots in the NBA that was able to speak.

Superstars

Many great players have suited up for the Warriors. A few of them have become icons of the team and the city it represents.

Paul Arizin

The Philadelphia Warriors selected Paul Azirin, a Philadelphia native, in the first round of the 1950 **NBA Draft**. He played two seasons for the Warriors before joining the United States Marines to fight in the Korean War. After his military service, Azirin rejoined the Warriors before the 1954–55 season. He was a member of the 1956 championship team that defeated the Fort Wayne Pistons in the NBA Finals. Azirin made 10 All-Star teams and averaged 22 points per game during his time in Philadelphia. He was inducted into the Basketball Hall of Fame in 1978.

Position: Forward/Guard
NBA Seasons: 10 (1950–1952 & 1954–1962)
Born: April 9, 1928, Philadelphia, Pennsylvania, United States

Wilt Chamberlain

Wilt Chamberlain signed with the Philadelphia Warriors before the 1959–60 season. In 1962, Chamberlain set an NBA record for scoring 100 points in a game against the New York Knicks. That record still stands today. He averaged 41 points and 25 rebounds per game over the course of his 6 seasons with the Warriors franchise. In 1960, Chamberlain won the NBA MVP Award and NBA Rookie of the Year Award. He made six All-Star teams along with four playoff appearances for the Warriors. In 1979, Chamberlain was inducted into the Basketball Hall of Fame.

Position: Center
NBA Seasons: 14 (1959–1973)
Born: August 21, 1936, Philadelphia, Pennsylvania, United States

Rick Barry

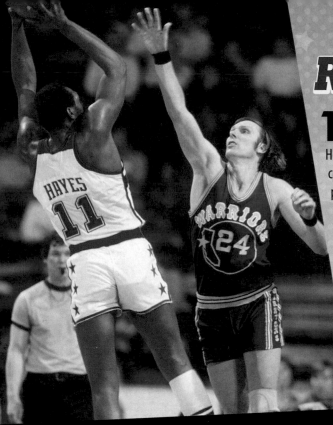

The San Francisco Warriors selected small forward Rick Barry with the second overall pick in the 1965 NBA Draft. He was NBA Rookie of the Year in 1966 and NBA scoring champ in 1967. After leaving the NBA for five seasons to play in the American Basketball Association (ABA), Barry rejoined the Golden State Warriors in 1972. He led the team to the 1975 NBA title and was named the NBA Finals MVP. Barry held averages 25 points, 7 rebounds, and 5 **assists** per game in 8 seasons with the Warriors. His legacy was enshrined into the Basketball Hall of Fame in 1987.

Position: Small Forward
NBA Seasons: 10 (1965–1967 & 1972–1980)
Born: March 28, 1944, Elizabeth, New Jersey, United States

Chris Mullin

Golden State selected Chris Mullin out of St. John's University in the first round of the 1985 NBA Draft. Along with guards Tim Hardaway and Mitch Richmond, Mullin was part of the memorable Warriors teams of the late 1980s. He made five NBA All-Star teams and one All-NBA First Team in 1992. In 13 seasons with Golden State, Mullin averaged 20 points per game. He made five postseason appearances with the Warriors, and won two Olympic Gold Medals with the U.S. Olympic Men's Basketball Team in 1984 and 1992. Mullin was inducted into the Basketball Hall of Fame in 2011.

Position: Small Forward and Shooting Guard
NBA Seasons: 16 (1985–2001)
Born: July 30, 1963, Brooklyn, New York, United States

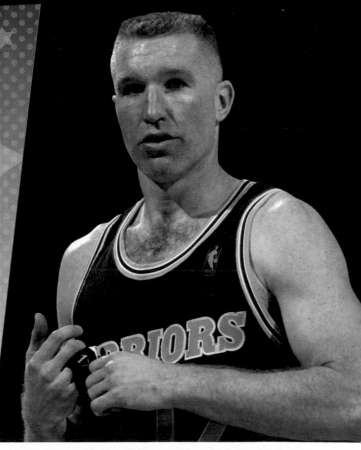

The Greatest of All Time

There are several standout players on the Warriors roster who have worked hard to push the team to success. Often, there is one player who has become known as the "Greatest of All Time," or GOAT. This player has gone above and beyond to achieve greatness and to help his team shine.

Stephen Curry

Position: Point Guard • **NBA Seasons:** 7 (2009–present)
Born: March 14, 1988, Akron, Ohio, United States

Stephen "Steph" Curry is the biggest superstar in the NBA today. He can shoot from anywhere and dribble circles around any defender. The Golden State Warriors selected Curry with the seventh overall pick in the 2009 NBA Draft. He was a member of the 2010 NBA All-Rookie First Team.

Curry made three All-Star teams from 2014 to 2016 and won the 2015 NBA MVP. He led the Warriors to the playoffs each year from 2013 to 2016. During the 2014–15 regular season, Curry averaged 23 points per game while shooting 44 percent from the three point line. In the 2015 playoffs, he averaged 28 points while shooting 42 percent from the three-point line. He capped off his MVP season by leading the team to its first NBA Championship since 1975.

In seven seasons in the NBA, Stephen Curry made 3,914 field goals.

At 151, Curry holds the record for most consecutive games with a three-pointer made.

fun facts

#1 During the 2015–16 season, Curry had a .908 **free throw** average.

#2 He has made three NBA All-Star teams.

#3 Curry has 40 Playoff game wins.

#4 As of 2016, he has made 1,593 three-pointers.

Stephen Curry helped the Warriors defeat the Cleveland Cavaliers in six games to claim the Larry O'Brien Championship Trophy in 2015.

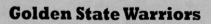

The Moment

The Golden State Warriors entered the 2015 Finals ranked first in defensive efficiency and second in offensive efficiency. These strengths led them to their fourth NBA title.

The greatest moment in Warriors history came during the 2015 NBA Finals. The franchise struggled for 20 seasons, but in 2014–15, the team was able to put together one of the most memorable seasons in NBA history. Golden State won 67 games during the regular season and cruised to the best record in the league.

Led by Curry, Klay Thompson, and Draymond Green, the team conquered the playoffs, losing only three games. The Warriors were set up to face the Cleveland Cavaliers in the 2015 NBA Finals. This meant that they would go up against LeBron James, one of the best basketball players in the NBA. The teams spilt the first two games in Oakland. Back in Cleveland, the Cavaliers won game 3. After the loss, the Warriors were in danger of letting their dream season slip away.

In game 4, the Warriors moved the ball on offense and shot well behind the three point line. Golden State crushed Cleveland by 21 points and sent the series back to Oakland tied at two. Golden State then won games 5 and 6 to earn the franchise's fourth NBA title and first since 1975.

Although James scored more points in the 2015 Finals, Curry had a higher scoring percentage, with .443 compared to James's .398.

After the win, the entire Golden State Warriors team ran onto the court in celebration.

All-Time Records

Highest Field Goal Percentage in a Season

63% During the 1994–95 season, Warriors forward Chris Gatling made 63 percent of his field goals. Gatling set the franchise **single-season record** for highest field goal percentage.

433

848
Most Assists in a Season
Warriors point guard Sleepy Floyd set the franchise single-season record for assists in 1986–87, with 848.

Most Defensive Rebounds in a Season
668 In 2012–13, Golden State power forward David Lee set the franchise single-season record for most defensive rebounds, with 668.

Most Offensive Rebounds in a Season

Warriors power forward Larry Smith holds the franchise single-season record for most offensive rebounds, with 433.

47%

Highest Three Point Field Goal Percentage in a Season

Warriors point guard B.J. Armstrong made a franchise single-season record 47 percent of his three pointers during the 1995–96 season.

345

Most Blocks in a Season

In 1988–89, Warriors center Manute Bol set the franchise single-season record for most **blocks**, with 345.

Timeline

Throughout the team's history, the Warriors have had many memorable events that have become defining moments for the team and its fans.

1946

The Warriors franchise is created. First known as the Philadelphia Warriors, the team is part of the Basketball Association of America (BAA).

1947

Led by coach Edward Gottlieb and power forward Joe Fulks, the Philadelphia Warriors win the 1947 BAA Championship. This title counts towards the Warrior's NBA title count because the BAA and NBA joined to create one league in the 1949 merger.

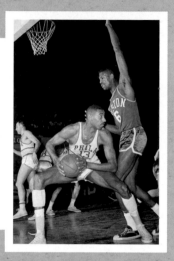

1950   1960   1970   1980

1962

Chamberlain scores 100 points in a single game as a member of the Warriors. The game is played in Hershey, Pennsylvania, against the New York Knicks. Chamberlain's final line from the game is 100 points and 25 rebounds. The record still stands to this day.

1975

Led by coach Al Attles and forwards Rick Barry and Jamaal Wilkes, the Golden State Warriors win the 1975 NBA Championship. This was the franchise's third NBA title.

1971

The team changes its name to the Golden State Warriors and adopts Oakland, California, as its new home city.

2006–2007

Don Nelson returns as head coach of the Warriors in June of 2006. Nelson and point guard Baron Davis lead Golden State to the 2007 Playoffs. As an eighth seed, the Warriors beat the top-seeded Dallas Mavericks in the first round of the playoffs.

2009

Golden State selects point guard Stephen Curry in the first round of the 2009 NBA Draft. Curry is now one the NBA's brightest stars and his selection changed the franchise's fortunes.

2011

The Warriors select sharpshooter Klay Thompson with the 11th overall pick in the 2011 NBA Draft. Shortly after, Thompson and Curry became known as the "Splash Brothers" for their ability to shoot from the outside.

| 1990 | 2000 | 2010 | 2020 |

2014–2015

Behind first year head coach Steve Kerr, the Warriors win 67 games in 2014–15. The team wins the 2015 NBA Finals against the Cleveland Cavaliers. The series win gives the franchise its fourth NBA title and first since 1975.

The Future

After coming up short against the Cleveland Cavaliers at the 2016 Finals, the Warriors are looking to repeat as NBA Champions moving forward. Curry and Thompson lead the team in scoring. Forwards Draymond Green and Harrison Barnes give the squad rebounding and defense, and Andrew Bogut provides toughness from the center position. The 2016 arrival of former Oklahoma City Thunder star, Kevin Durant, only adds to the depth of the Warriors' team.

Write a Biography

Life Story

A person's life story can be the subject of a book. This kind of book is called a biography. Biographies often describe the lives of people who have achieved great success. These people may be alive today, or they may have lived many years ago. Reading a biography can help you learn more about a great person.

Get the Facts

Use this book, and research in the library and on the internet, to find out more about your favorite star. Learn as much about this player as you can. What position does he play? What are his statistics in important categories? Has he set any records? Also, be sure to write down key events in the person's life. What was his childhood like? What has he accomplished off the court? Is there anything else that makes this person special or unusual?

Use the Concept Web

A concept web is a useful research tool. Read the questions in the concept web on the following page. Answer the questions in your notebook. Your answers will help you write a biography.

Concept Web

Your Opinion
- What did you learn from the books you read in your research?
- Would you suggest these books to others?
- Was anything missing from these books?

Adulthood
- Where does this individual currently reside?
- Does he or she have a family?

Childhood
- Where and when was this person born?
- Describe his or her parents, siblings, and friends.
- Did this person grow up in unusual circumstances?

Write a Biography

Accomplishments off the Court
- What is this person's life's work?
- Has he or she received awards or recognition for accomplishments?
- How have this person's accomplishments served others?

Help and Obstacles
- Did this individual have a positive attitude?
- Did he or she receive help from others?
- Did this person have a mentor?
- Did this person face any hardships?
- If so, how were the hardships overcome?

Accomplishments on the Court
- What records does this person hold?
- What key games and plays have defined his career?
- What are his stats in categories important to his position?

Work and Preparation
- What was this person's education?
- What was his or her work experience?
- How does this person work?
- What is the process he or she uses?

Trivia Time

Take this quiz to test your knowledge of the Golden State Warriors.
The answers are printed upside down under each question.

1 Where do the Warriors currently play their home games?

A. Oracle Arena

2 How many regular-season games did the Warriors win in 2014–15?

A. 67

3 When did the Philadelphia Warriors join the NBA?

A. 1949

4 Which pick did the Warriors select Stephen Curry with in the 2009 NBA Draft?

A. Seventh overall

5 Which team did the Warriors defeat in the 2015 NBA Finals?

A. Cleveland Cavaliers

6 When did Stephen Curry win the NBA MVP Award?

A. 2015

7 Which team did the Warriors upset in the 2007 NBA Playoffs?

A. Dallas Mavericks

8 How many defensive rebounds did David Lee have in 2012–13?

A. 668

9 When did the Warriors move to California?

A. 1962

10 What year did Wilt Chamberlain score 100 points in a game?

A. 1962

11 What position did Rick Barry play?

A. Small forward

12 Where did Chris Mullin go to college?

A. St. John's University

Key Words

assists: a statistic that is attributed to up to two players of the scoring team who shoot, pass, or deflect the ball toward the scoring teammate

blocks: when a defensive player taps an offensive player's shot out of the air and stops it from getting to the basket

conference: an association of sports teams that play each other

franchise: a team that is a member of a professional sports league

free throw: open or undefended shot at the basket taken from the foul line, also called foul shots

logo: a symbol that stands for a team or organization

NBA Draft: the annual event in June where NBA teams select players from college to join the league. Teams select in order based on the prior season's winning percentages.

playoffs: a series of games that occur after regular season play

rebounds: taking possession of the ball after missed shots

single-season record: a record set in a specific category for a franchise during an individual season

Index

Log on to www.av2books.com

AV² by Weigl brings you media enhanced books that support active learning. Go to www.av2books.com, and enter the special code found on page 2 of this book. You will gain access to enriched and enhanced content that supplements and complements this book. Content includes video, audio, weblinks, quizzes, a slide show, and activities.

AV² Online Navigation

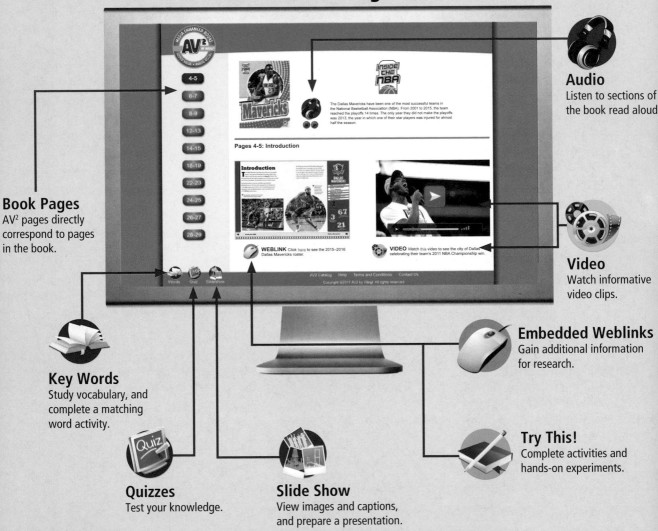

Book Pages
AV² pages directly correspond to pages in the book.

Key Words
Study vocabulary, and complete a matching word activity.

Quizzes
Test your knowledge.

Slide Show
View images and captions, and prepare a presentation.

Audio
Listen to sections of the book read aloud.

Video
Watch informative video clips.

Embedded Weblinks
Gain additional information for research.

Try This!
Complete activities and hands-on experiments.

AV² was built to bridge the gap between print and digital. We encourage you to tell us what you like and what you want to see in the future.

Sign up to be an AV² Ambassador at www.av2books.com/ambassador.